AWESOME JOKES

AWESOME
JOKES

Packed full
of great gags
and classic
chuckles!

ARCTURUS

ARCTURUS

This edition published in 2012 by Arcturus Publishing Limited
26/27 Bickels Yard, 151–153 Bermondsey Street,
London SE1 3HA

ISBN: 978-1-84837-626-7
CH001570EN
Supplier 16, Date 0412, Print Run 1652

Author: Kay Barnham
Illustrations: Quadrum
Design and layout: Moseley Strachan

Printed in Singapore

CONTENTS

Get ready to giggle! It's chuckle time!

Prepare for your sides to split, your eyes to water and your tummy to wobble like the wobbliest jelly ever with hysterical laughter. It will be worse than being tickled! Much worse...

This book is full of the silliest, craziest and most amusing jokes around. There's something for everyone. From knock, knock jokes to classic chuckles, you'll have your friends and family in stitches for hours... days... years... centuries! You'll soon be known as the funniest person in the world.

Take a deep breath and prepare for the best jokes ever! You and your friends will laugh so loudly everyone will want to join in.

CHEEKY CRITTERS

Which side of a hedgehog is the sharpest?
The outside.

What do cats like to watch on television?
The evening mews.

Why was the glow-worm disappointed?
Because her children weren't very bright.

What do birds eat for breakfast?
Tweetabix.

What do cats eat for breakfast?
Mice Krispies.

What do sheep do when the weather's hot?
Have a baa-baa-cue.

What do you get if you point a hairdryer
down a rabbit hole?
Hot cross bunnies.

What did the grape say when the elephant
stepped on him?
Nothing. He just let out a little wine.

Why do giraffes have such long necks?
Because they have very smelly feet.

What goes 'oom oom'?
A cow walking backwards.

What do you get if you cross a dinosaur
with a tea party?
A tyrannosaucer.

What's an elephant's favourite game?
Squash.

Why are wolves like playing cards?
They come in packs.

What name did the snail give to his home?
Michelle.

What's got a hundred legs and can see just as
well from both ends?
A centipede with its eyes shut.

What's green, cold-blooded and follows
the yellow brick road?
The Lizard of Oz.

What's the difference between a fly and a bird?
A bird can fly but a fly can't bird.

What's the difference between a weasel
and a stoat?
**A weasel is weasily recognisable and a stoat
is stoatily different!**

What does a cat rest its head on at night?
A caterpillow.

What's white, furry and smells of peppermint?
A Polo bear.

What's worse than raining cats and dogs?
Hailing taxis.

Where do sharks come from?
Finland.

Where do you find an upside-down tortoise?
Where you left it.

What has three legs and goes "hee-haw"?
A wonky donkey.

Where do insects do their shopping?
In a flea market.

When can three elephants get under an
umbrella and not get wet?
When it isn't raining.

What's a crocodile's favourite card game?
Snap.

What did the pig say when the farmer
grabbed him by the tail?
"That's the end of me!"

What do you call a cat who swallows a duck?
A duck-filled fatty-puss.

What do you call a sleeping bull?
A bulldozer.

What do you get if you walk under a cow?
A pat on the head.

What time is it when an elephant
sits on your bike?
Time to get a new bike.

What happened to the cat who
swallowed a ball of wool?
She had mittens.

What do you get from a nervous cow?
Milkshakes.

What goes black-white-black-white-black-
white?
A penguin rolling down a hill.

Why do pet shops always sell out of birds
before any other animal?
Because they go cheep.

What should you never do with an
angry rhinoceros?
Argue.

What is a hedgehog's favourite snack?
Prickled onions.

How can you tell that carrots help you
see in the dark?
Have you ever seen a rabbit with a torch?

Why is there no point playing jokes on snakes?
You can't pull their legs.

What should you do if you find a gorilla
sleeping in your bed?
Sleep somewhere else!

My dog's a blacksmith.
How can I tell?
**When I tell him off, he makes
a bolt for the door.**

Which dogs love to have their hair washed?
Shampoodles.

What is a cat's favourite party game?
Mewsical chairs.

Where do horses and ponies live?
In the neighbourhood.

Did you hear about the crocodile
with the camera?
He was snap-happy.

Why did the lion spit out the clown?
Because he tasted funny.

Why didn't the prawn like to share?
Because it was a little shellfish.

Why do birds fly south in the winter?
Because it's too far to walk.

Why do bees have sticky hair?
Because they use honeycombs.

What do caterpillars do on New Year's Day?
Turn over a new leaf.

What do frogs wear on their feet in summer?
Open-toad sandals.

What's grey and has four legs and a trunk?
A mouse going on holiday.

Why did the tiny terrier puppy
bite people's ankles?
He couldn't reach any higher.

Why do lions eat raw meat?
Because they don't know how to use ovens.

What do you call a snake that travels
around on the front of a car?
A windscreen viper.

What animal loves a good novel?
A bookworm.

What happened when the tortoise
collided with the terrapin?
It was a turtle disaster.

What did the police officer say when
the spider ran down his back?
You're under a vest!

How do you stop a rhinoceros from charging?
Take away its credit cards.

What type of cows eat grass?
Lawn moo-ers.

What's a snake's favourite subject?
Hisssstory.

What's a snake's favourite subject?
Hisssstory.

Why do leopards make rubbish thieves?
They are always spotted.

What did one sheep say to the other sheep?
"After ewe."

How do you get down from a camel?
You don't. You get down from a goose.

Where does a monkey make toast?
Under a gorilla.

How did the puppy stop the DVD?
He used paws.

How do chicks get out of their shells?
They eggs-it.

What does a cat do when it gets angry?
It goes up the wall.

What do whales eat for dinner?
Fish and ships.

What do you give a poorly pig?
Oinkment.

What happens when two snails have a fight?
They slug it out.

SEASIDE
SILLINESS

What is a fish's favourite party game?
Tide-and-seek.

Who lives in a sandcastle?
A sandwitch.

What did the blue whale say when he collided
with the bottlenose dolphin?
"I didn't do it on porpoise."

What are the strongest creatures in the ocean?
Mussels.

Why are dolphins cleverer than humans?
They can train a human to stand at the side of a pool and throw fish to them.

What's the difference between
a fish and a piano?
You can't tuna fish.

What happens when you throw a
purple rock into the Red Sea?
It gets wet.

Why can't penguins fly?
They can't afford aeroplane tickets.

What did the seaweed say when it was stuck to
the bottom of the speedboat?
"Kelp!!!!!"

What do penguins have for lunch?
Icebergers.

Where do you weigh a whale?
At a whale-weigh station.

What's the best way to catch a fish?
Get someone to throw it at you.

Which is the shiniest fish in the sea?
The starfish.

What is a sailor's favourite colour?
Navy blue.

What's the fastest thing in the sea?
A motor-pike.

Where did the ship go when it
was feeling poorly?
It visited the docks.

What's yellow and dangerous?
Shark-infested custard.

Why was the pupil's school report wet?
Because her grades were all below C level.

Why do fish avoid computers?
They don't want to get caught in the internet.

How did the tiny shellfish cross the seabed?
By taxi crab.

What happened when the boat carrying blue
paint hit the boat carrying red paint?
All of the passengers were marooned.

What's black, incredibly rude and
floats on water?
Crude oil.

What lives under the sea and carries
lots of people to and fro?
An octo-bus.

Why did the fish take such a long time
to make his mind up?
He wanted to mullet over.

What do you get if you cross a fish with
an elephant?
Swimming trunks.

Who do fish borrow money from?
A loan shark.

Why are seagulls called seagulls?
**Because if they flew over bays, they
would be bagels.**

Who dresses like a cowboy and lives
in the ocean?
Billy the Squid.

What's the best way to get in touch with a fish?
Drop it a line.

Which is the saddest creature in the sea?
The blue whale.

Why are fish easy to weigh?
They have their own scales.

What's a carpenter's favourite sea creature?
A hammerhead shark.

Why don't you ever see penguins near the UK?
They're scared of Wales.

Which sea creatures are the biggest cry babies?
Whales.

What do you find on very small beaches?
Microwaves.

What does an octopus wear in the winter?
A coat of arms.

Where do very young fish go every morning?
Plaice school.

Who was the first underwater spy?
James Pond.

Why wasn't the girl scared when
a shark swam past her?
It was a man-eating shark.

What do you give a deaf fish?
A herring aid.

Why did the sailor carry a piece of
rope on to the boat?
Because he was the skipper.

How do cod and mackerel watch the news?
On a telefishon.

What do the ocean and a Christmas pudding
have in common?
They're both full of currents!

What do you find in the middle
of the ocean?
The letter "e".

What do you find in the middle of the ocean?

Why didn't the sea captain's radio
work in rough seas?
It was on the wrong wavelength.

What do you get if you cross a snowman
and a shark?
Frostbite.

What's a pirate's favourite letter
of the alphabet?
R.

How much did the pirate pay for his wooden leg
and terrifyingly sharp hook?
An arm and a leg.

Why did the crab blush?
Because the seaweed.

Why did the animal welfare officer close
down the fish and chip shop?
They were battering the fish.

What does a bridegroom wear to an
underwater wedding?
A very wet suit.

What's green and knobbly and spends
a lot of time under the sea?
An avocado wearing scuba gear.

LAUGHS
OUT LOUD

Why did the chicken cross the road?
To get to the other side.

Why did the pterodactyl cross the road?
Because chickens didn't exist then.

Why did Captain Hook cross the road?
To get to the second hand shop.

How many chickens does it take to
change a lightbulb?
None, they're all too busy crossing the road.

A girl walks into a shop and says,
"I'd like to buy a wasp, please."
"But we don't sell any wasps,"
says the shopkeeper.
"That's funny," says the girl.
"You have one in your window."

How many babysitters does it take
to change a lightbulb?
None. Lightbulbs don't wear nappies.

What happened when Tinkerbell flew
backwards and forwards between
Dover and Calais?
She was a cross-channel fairy.

Why did the chicken cross the road, jump
in a muddy ditch and cross back
over the road again?
Because he was a dirty double-crosser.

What's black and white and noisy?
A zebra with a drum.

What begins with "e" and ends with "e"
and has a letter in the middle?
An envelope.

Knock knock.
Who's there?
Scott.
Scott who?
Scott nothing to do with you!

Why is tap dancing dangerous?
If you slip, you might fall in the sink!

Did you hear about the magical tractor?
It turned into a field.

What's black and white and black
and white and green?
Two zebras fighting over a pickled gherkin.

What's green and goes camping?
A Brussels scout.

Knock knock.
Who's there?
A lass.
A lass who?
Isn't that what cowboys use?

What's black and white and eats like a horse?
A zebra.

39

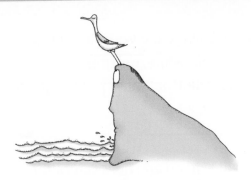

What do you call a man with a seagull
on his head?
Cliff.

What do you call a deer with no eyes?
No idea.

What do you call a deer with no eyes
who's totally motionless?
Still no idea.

What do you call a deer with no eyes who's
totally motionless and is on fire?
Still flaming no idea.

What's grey, yellow, white, grey,
yellow, white and grey?
**An elephant rolling down the hill
with a daisy in its mouth.**

Knock knock.
Who's there?
Doris.
Doris who?
Doris locked. That's why I had to knock!

Knock knock.
Who's there?
Tank.
Tank who?
You're welcome!

What should you feed an elf who
wants to be taller?
Elf-raising flour.

Knock knock.
Who's there?
Boo.
Boo who?
Don't cry. It's only a joke.

Knock knock.
Who's there?
Hawaii.
Hawaii who?
I'm fine, thanks. How are you?

Did you hear about the woman with the big fluffy hat called Cynthia?
That's a funny name for a hat.

How many police officers does it take to screw in a lightbulb?
None. It turned itself in.

Knock knock.
Who's there?
Ya.
Ya who?
What are you getting so excited about?

Why did the code-breaker spend so long in
the percussion section of the orchestra?
He was looking for cymbals.

What do you call a man with a car on his head?
Jack.

Knock knock.
Who's there?
Norma Lee.
Norma Lee who?
Norma Lee I'd ring the doorbell.

What do you call a man with rabbits
in his trousers?
Warren.

What type of dog can tell the time?
A watchdog.

What do you call a tree with a croaky voice?
A hoarse chestnut.

What is an archaeologist?
Someone whose career is in ruins.

What is an archaeologist?

Have you heard the joke about the bed?
No, I haven't. How does it go?
Sorry, it hasn't been made up yet.

Where do pianists go on holiday?
The Florida Keys.

How do you keep a total idiot in suspense?
I'll tell you later.

What do you call a man who can't stand up?
Neil.

Knock, knock.
Who's there?
Dishes.
Dishes who?
Dishes a terrible joke!

Did you hear about the tax dodger
who got into hot water?
The cold tap was broken.

How does a policeman listen to music
on the beat?
On his iPlod.

How does Jack Frost travel?
By icicle.

What's hairy and sneezes?
A coconut with a cold.

What did the scarf say to the hat?
You go on ahead and I'll just hang around.

How many shop assistants does it take to
change a lightbulb?
One, as long as you have the receipt.

If you found money in every pocket of your
trousers, what would you have?
Someone else's trousers.

Why did the man bash the
giggling fortune teller?
He was striking a happy medium.

What do you get when you cross a dog
with an elephant?
A really nervous postman.

What do you call a camel with three humps?
Humphrey.

Why are management meetings always
so horribly dull?
They're held in the Bored Room.

Did you hear about the man who went
to sleep under the leaky, old car?
He wanted to wake up oily in the morning.

FUNNY
FOOD

How do Welsh people eat cheese?
Caerphilly.

Why is an old-fashioned radio like roasted pork?
They both have lots of crackling.

How do you make a chicken stew?
Keep it waiting for a couple of hours.

What's orange and points North?
A magnetic carrot.

How do you make a Mexican chilli?
Send him to Siberia.

How do you make a sausage roll?
Push it down a hill.

What do snowmen eat for breakfast?
Snowflakes.

Why did the rhubarb go out with a prune?
Because he couldn't find a date.

How do you make an apple puff?
Chase it round the kitchen.

Why did the tomato go red?
Because it saw the salad dressing.

Why is a Brussels sprout small and green?
**Because if it was big and red it would
be a fire engine.**

How do you make a fruit punch?
Give it boxing lessons.

What type of cheese is made backwards?
Edam.

Did you hear about the elf who ate too fast?
He was goblin his food.

What noise does a nut make when it sneezes?
"Cashew!"

What kind of room can you eat?
A mushroom.

Which fruit never ever gets lonely?
A pear.

What did the Hungarian ghost eat for dinner?
Ghoulash.

Why did the bacon laugh?
Because the egg cracked a yolk.

What do elves make sandwiches with?
Shortbread.

How do you make hot chocolate?
Leave it out in the sun.

What's the best thing to put in a chocolate bar?
Your teeth.

What wobbles as it flies?
A jellycopter.

What do red squirrels eat?
Gingernuts.

Did you hear about the chocolate-coated train?
It was a cocoa-motive.

What did the classical musician love to eat?
Organ-ic chocolate.

What is the highest pudding in Paris?
The Trifle Tower

What happens if you eat Christmas
decorations?
You get tinselitis.

What did the sherbert say to the humbug?
"Hi, sweetie!"

Why did the cream squeal?
Someone was whipping it.

What did the teddy bear say when he
was offered second helpings?
"No, thanks. I'm stuffed!"

What's yellow and stupid?
Thick custard.

Why did the jelly wobble?
Because it saw the milk shake.

How do you make a glass of milkshake?
Give it a fright.

Why did the schoolboy eat his homework?
The teacher told him it was a piece of cake.

😊

What do you get if you put five ducks in a box?
A box of quackers.

😊

What's a cannibal's favourite takeaway?
Pizza with everyone on it.

😊

Why did the man eat at the investment bank?
He loved rich food.

😊

What's the best thing to put in an apple pie?
A spoon.

😊

What did one plate say to the other plate?
"Lunch is on me!"

Why didn't the boy with a sausage up his nose
and a chocolate bar in his ear feel well?
He wasn't eating properly.

What did the waiter say when the horse walked
into the café?
"Why the long face?"

How did the banana know he was ill?
He wasn't peeling well.

How do you turn light chocolate
into dark chocolate?
Turn the light off.

☺

Did you hear about the fruit salad
without any pink fruit in it?
It was peachless.

☺

What's small, green and round and
goes up, down, up, down?
A pea in a lift.

☺

Why couldn't the poppy seed leave
the bowling alley?
Because he was on a roll.

☺

Where do people swap jugs of gravy
with each other?
At the Stock Exchange.

Have you heard the joke about the butter?
**Sorry, I can't tell you because
you might spread it.**

What did the egg in the monastery say?
"Out of the frying pan, into the friar!"

What did the speedy tomato
say to the slow tomato?
"Ketchup!"

What do you call an aeroplane passenger
covered in salt and pepper?
A seasoned traveller.

What happened to the hyena who
accidentally swallowed an OXO cube?
He became a laughing stock.

What do you call a worried turnip?
An edgy veggie.

What happened to the rhubarb thief?
He ended up in custody.

What does the queen do when she burps?
Issues a royal pardon.

What's worse than biting into an apple
and finding a worm?
Finding half a worm.

What is small, round and can't help laughing?
A tickled onion.

Where do fish keep their savings?
In riverbanks.

What did the baby corn say to the mama corn?
Where's the pop corn?

Who solved the sweet-shop mystery?
Sherbert Holmes.

Where do monkeys sleep?
In ape-ricots.

What's round, shiny and says "ahem"?
A cough sweet.

SCHOOL FOOLERY

What do elves do after school?
Gnomework.

What did the set square say to the protractor?
"Take me to your ruler."

How do you fix a broken tuba?
With a tubaglue.

Why do learner witches need dictionaries?
They can't spell.

What did the o say to the 8?
"Cool belt."

What do IT teachers eat for dinner?
Chips.

If the red house was made of red bricks and the brown house was made of brown bricks, what was the green house made of?
Glass.

How did the Vikings send secret messages during lessons?
By Norse Code.

What was the dog awarded when he left university?
A pedigree.

Which tree has square roots?
A geometry.

What's purple and burns?
The Grape Fire of London.

Which building always has the most storeys?
A library.

Why did the girl go to night school?
**Because she wanted to learn to
read in the dark.**

What are you going to be
when you leave school?
Older.

Did you hear about the cowboy who
helped run the school?
He was the deputy head.

Did you hear about the schoolboy who was
asked to use the word "fascinate" in a sentence?
**He said, "I've got ten buttons on my
cardigan, but I can only fasten eight!"**

What is an insect's best subject at school?
Mothematics.

What did Henry VIII become on
his 21st birthday?
A year older.

What's the fruitiest lesson at school?
History. It's full of dates.

What's the longest sentence ever?
Life imprisonment.

What do really tiny IT teachers eat for dinner?
Microchips.

What do you call a Roman emperor with a cold?
Julius Sneezer.

What kind of lighting did Noah use for his ark?
Floodlights.

Why did the Romans build straight roads?
So they didn't go round the bend.

What's the longest word in the world?
"Smiles", because there's a mile between the first letter and the last.

Where do bad spellers look up words?
In a dickshunerry.

Where was the Magna Carta signed?
At the bottom.

Which snake is good at sums?
An adder.

What did the headteacher say
to the naughty egg?
"You're eggspelled."

What's the fastest way to double your money?
Fold it in half.

What kind of meals do geometry teachers
enjoy?
Square meals.

Where does success come before work?
In a dictionary.

What's the capital of Peru?
P.

☺

Who invented King Arthur's round table?
Sir Cumference.

☺

Which month has 28 days?
All of them.

☺

What is adding?
It's the noise a doorbell makes.

☺

Why did the teacher put the lights on?
Because the class was dim.

☺

What's a maths teacher's favourite meal?
Pi.

What is a polygon?
A dead parrot.

Which schooldays start with the letter T?
Today and tomorrow.

Why did Henry VIII have so many wives?
He liked to chop and change.

What do elves learn at school?
The elf-abet.

Which word is always spelt incorrectly?
Incorrectly.

How do pupils get straight As?
By using a ruler.

Why did the teacher wear sunglasses?
Because his class was so bright.

How do bees get to school?
On the buzz.

Where did Noah keep his oldest bees?
In the ark hive.

What comes before 11?
The postman.

Why is Europe like a dirty frying pan?
Because it has Greece at the bottom.

Why was the school girl excited?
**Because the teacher had told her
to wait there for the present.**

Why was the music teacher
locked out of his classroom?
The keys were on the piano.

Why was Elizabeth I buried
at Westminster Abbey?
Because she was dead.

Why was the school cook arrested?
**Because she beat the eggs and
whipped the cream.**

What do you get if you cross a vampire
and a teacher?
Blood tests.

Have you heard the joke about the blunt pencil?
No, I haven't. What is it?
Sorry, I can't tell you. There's no point.

Why did the school cook get a shock?
**He stepped on a teacake and a
currant went up his leg.**

What do we do with crude oil?
Teach it good manners.

Who invented fractions?
Henry the Eighth.

Why was Rome built at night?
Because it wasn't built in a day.

What was Camelot famous for?
Its knight life.

Where was Queen Elizabeth II crowned?
On her head.

Why is six scared of seven?
Because seven ate nine.

COSMIC
CAPERS

What did the alien say to the petrol pump?
**"It's very rude to stick your finger
in your ear when I'm talking to you!"**

😊

Where do you find black holes?
In black socks.

😊

What do you call an overweight alien?
An extra-cholesterol.

😊

What do aliens rest their teacups on?
Flying saucers.

What did Venus say to Saturn?
"Why not give me a ring sometime?"

🙂

What's big, bright, round and very, very silly?
A fool moon.

🙂

What did the alien say to the plant?
"Take me to your weeder."

🙂

What's ET short for?
Because he has little legs.

🙂

Where do aliens go to build sandcastles?
The galax-seaside.

🙂

Which star is the most dangerous?
The shooting star.

What's the centre of gravity?
The letter V.

Why did the alien spacecraft land
outside the bedroom door?
The landing light was on.

What happened when the astrophysicist
slammed his front door?
There was a Big Bang.

How many astronomers
does it take to change a lightbulb?
None. They prefer the dark.

How do astronomers know that
the universe isn't heavy?
Because distances are measured in light years.

What type of songs do planets love to hear?
Nep-tunes.

Where does Dr Who buy his sundried tomatoes?
At a dalekatessen.

Did you hear about the man who was
whisked away by alien teddy bears?
He had a close encounter of the furred kind.

Why did the astrophysicist fit a knocker
on his front door?
He wanted to win the No Bell Prize.

Did you hear about the supersonic egg?
It couldn't be beaten.

What did the Metric alien say to the human?
"Take me to your litre."

What did the NASA astronaut wear?
Apollo-neck jumper.

Why are parties on the moon always rubbish?
There's no atmosphere

What's the easiest way to
experience time travel?
Throw your clock at the wall.

What do you get if you cross
Earth's atmosphere with a hot drink?
Gravi-tea.

Which astronaut wears the
biggest space helmet?
The one with the biggest head.

How do you know if the spaceship's
engine is running?
You have to run after it.

What do spacemen play when
they're orbiting Earth?
Astronauts and crosses.

Did you hear about the cashew
who went into orbit?
He was an astronut.

If meteorites collide with planets,
what do you call meteorites that miss?
Meteowrongs.

How does the Solar System hold up its trousers?
With an asteroid belt.

What's the most important thing to do if you're
going to have a party in space?
Plan-et.

Why don't astronauts get hungry until they've
been in space for a few hours?
They've just had a big launch.

What totally bonkers insect lives on the moon?
A lunar-tick.

What kind of poems do you find in outer space?
Uni-verse.

Why don't astronauts take eggs into space?
Because eggs're terrestrial.

How do you get a baby astronaut to go to sleep?
Rocket.

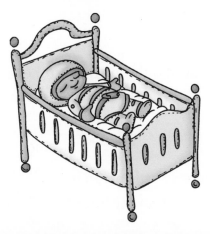

Which star wears dark glasses?
A film star.

What type of astronaut can jump higher
than a house?
All of them – houses can't jump.

How did the aliens hurt the farmer?
They landed on his corn.

Where do little green men get their eggs?
From the little green hen.

When do astronauts eat?
At launch time.

Which is the most precious planet?
Saturn. It has a lot of rings.

Which do you put on a space horse?
A saddle-lite.

What do aliens cook their breakfast on?
An unidentified frying object.

How did the alien tie his shoelaces?
With an astroknot.

What holds the moon up?
Moon beams.

What did one asteroid say to the other asteroid?
"Pleased to meteor."

What does the man in the moon
use instead of plates?
Satellite dishes.

How does the barber cut the man
in the moon's hair?
E-clipse it.

What do you call a spaceship with
a faulty thermostat?
A frying saucer.

Why was the thirsty astronaut loitering near
the computer keyboard?
He was looking for the space bar.

GRINS AND GIGGLES

How do you get rid of varnish?
Take away the "r"!

Did you hear about the embarrassed toilet?
It was flushed.

Why were the Middle Ages so dark?
Because there were so many knights.

How can you make your money go a long way?
Put your piggy bank in a rocket.

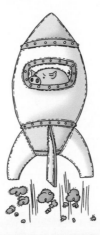

What do the letter A and
a rose have in common?
Bs come after them both.

What do snowmen sing at parties?
"Freeze a jolly good fellow..."

Did you hear about the man who
was mad about tractors one day,
but bored of them the next?
He had become an ex-tractor fan.

What's the difference between a crossword
whizz and an old lady with a sweet tooth?
**One is a good puzzler and the
other is a pud guzzler.**

What's brown and sticky?
A stick.

What do cats put in their drinks?
Mice cubes.

What wears shoes but has no feet?
The pavement.

Why did the girl take the pencil to bed with her?
She wanted to draw the curtains.

What's a top night out for a geologist?
A rock concert.

What sits on the seabed and shakes?
A nervous wreck.

What's the fastest cake in the world?
Scone.

Why do rabbits have fur coats?
Because they'd look daft in leather jackets.

Did you hear about the actor
who fell through the floor?
It was just a stage he was going through.

What's the difference between a
well-dressed gentleman and
an exhausted dog?
**One wears a posh suit and
the other just pants.**

How do trees get on the internet?
They log in.

How do you make a bandstand?
Take away their seats.

What do refuse collectors eat?
Junk food.

What did the lovestruck stamp
say to the envelope?
"I'm stuck on you."

How do you turn soup into gold?
Add 24 carrots.

How do you join the girl guides?
Rope them all together.

What is full of holes, but can still hold water?
A sponge.

What's the capital of England?
E.

When do lorry drivers stop for a snack?
When they see a fork in the road.

Why are elephants all wrinkly?
Have you ever tried to iron one?

What did the sink say to the leaky tap?
"You're a drip."

Which is the tiredest part of a car?
The exhaust pipe.

What has four wheels and flies?
A garbage truck.

What do you call a judge with no thumbs?
Justice Fingers.

Why did James Bond have a lie-in?
He was an undercover agent.

What's round and dangerous?
A vicious circle.

Who works at MI5 over the Christmas holidays?
Mince spies.

When is a car not a car?
When it turns into a garage.

When is a car not a car?

Where did the king keep his armies?
Up his sleevies.

Why did the man wear a banana skin
on each foot?
He wanted a pair of slippers.

Where does Tarzan buy
second-hand underpants?
At a jungle sale.

What do you get if you cross Count Dracula
with Sir Lancelot?
A bite in shining armour.

What has a long tail, colourful feathers and
wears a bow?
A birthday pheasant.

What did the big candle say to the little candle?
"You're too young to go out."

☺

Who stole the sponge from the bathroom?
The robber duck.

☺

Why did the belt go to prison?
Because it held up a pair of trousers.

☺

What flavour squash do monsters slurp?
Lemon and slime.

☺

What's pink and fluffy?
Pink fluff.

☺

What's blue and fluffy?
Pink fluff holding its breath.

What do you get if you cross a sheep
with a trampoline?
A woolly jumper.

What do Rupert The Bear and Winnie
The Pooh have in common?
They both have the same middle name.

What do you call a boomerang
that doesn't come back?
A stick.

What did the Spanish firefighter
call his twin sons?
José and Hose B.

What do you call two robbers
dressed in ladies' underwear?
A pair of nickers.

What can you always count on?
Your fingers.

How can you walk through walls?
Open the door.

What's green and smells of yellow paint?
Green paint.

What did Cinderella say when her photos
weren't ready on time?
"Some day my prints will come."

What sound do hedgehogs make
when they hug?
"Ouch!"

What do you get if you cross a painter and
decorator with a police officer?
A brush with the law.

What do you call a man with a purply-browny-
yellowy mark on his forehead?
Bruce.

What do you get if you cross a kangaroo
with a sheep?
A woolly jumper with pockets.

What do you get if you cross a snake
with a builder?
A boa constructor.

GAMES FOR A LAUGH

What's striped, furry and goes
"meeeeeowwwwwww"?
A cat in a racing car.

Did you hear about the Formula One car
with a wooden engine?
It wooden go.

How do Formula One witches travel?
By vroomstick.

What should a football team do
if the pitch is flooded?
Bring on their subs.

What do you get if you cross a bunch of
crazy jokers with a football team?
Mad Jester United.

What do you call a pig that does karate?
A pork chop.

What's the fastest vegetable on earth?
A runner bean.

Why are goalkeepers stinking rich?
Because they are good savers.

Where do footballers go dancing?
At a football.

Why was the pirate such an amazing boxer?
Because of his left hook.

What did the cricket glove say
to the cricket ball?
"Catch you later!"

What happened when the monkey
scored a goal?
The crowd went bananas.

How do you start a teddy bear race?
"Ready, teddy, go!"

Why did the ambulance arrive on the football
pitch after 90 minutes were up?
The players were into injury time.

☺

Do undersea creatures play football?
**Yes, they do. There are
20,000 Leagues Under the Sea.**

☺

What happened to the football player
who wore perfume?
He was scent off.

☺

Did you hear about the sticky,
see-through football player?
He was a transfer.

☺

Who can spot promising players and tie
seventeen different types of knot?
A scout.

Why was the computer such a terrific golfer?
It had a hard drive.

Did you hear about the rugby-mad
monster with nine heads?
He had nine caps.

Did you hear about the scarecrow
who won a gold medal?
He was out standing in his field.

Did you hear about the sports equipment
manufacturer with his stereo on full blast?
He was making a racket.

What did Robin Hood say when he was
almost hit at the archery tournament?
"That was an arrow escape!"

What kind of cats are great at bowling?
Alley cats.

What do you get if you cross a football team
with a tub of ice cream?
Aston Vanilla.

If marathon runners suffer from athlete's foot,
what do soldiers suffer from?
Missile toe.

What did the parachuting insect shout as
it jumped out of the aeroplane?
"Earwig go!"

Which insect was terrible in goal?
The fumblebee.

Why did the basketball players spin the ball on their fingertips?
Because it was the Whirled Cup.

Why did the football player kick the ball around his own back garden?
It was a home game.

What's a horse's favourite sport?
Stable tennis.

How do you know when a referee is
having a smashing time?
He whistles while he works.

What do babies and football players
have in common?
They're both really good at dribbling.

If there's a referee in football,
what is there in bowls?
Soup!

Did you hear about the monk
who longed to be a football player?
He was trying to kick the habit.

In which league do French fries play football?
In the Premierchip.

What is a marathon runner's favourite subject?
Jography.

Where do old bowling balls get thrown?
In the gutter.

What's the angriest part of a goal?
The crossbar.

What's the hungriest part of a goal?
The goalmouth.

What do you call a really tiny sports' fan?
A speck-tator.

What's a footballer's favourite pudding?
Pitch melba.

Which part of a rugby stadium
never stays the same?
The changing rooms.

Why wouldn't the football player
cross the road?
It was offside.

Why was Cinderella a terrible football player?
Because her coach was a pumpkin.

What's green and runs around the garden?
A hedge.

😊

Why was the tennis court wet?
Because of the floodlights.

😊

Why do basketball players love biscuits?
They can dunk them.

😊

How do you start a jelly race?
"Get set!"

😊

Why did the runner never forget anything?
He was always jogging his memory.

😊

Why is it sweltering hot after a football match?
All the fans have gone home.

MONSTER
MISCHIEF

Why should witches never lose their tempers
while they're zooming around on a broomstick?
They would fly off the handle.

What's the best way to speak
to a scary monster?
Long-distance.

What do you call a dinosaur
wearing a blindfold?
Doyouthinkhesaurus.

Where do ghosts live?
At the dead end.

What does the headless horseman ride?
A night mare.

How do you make a witch itch?
Take away the "w"!

What do trainee witches do at school?
Spelling tests.

Why don't witches get sunburnt?
They use suntan potion.

Did you hear about the overweight witch?
She went to Weight Witches.

Where do ghouls go on holiday?
The Ghosta Brava.

😊

Why was the ghost so hilarious?
He was dead funny.

😊

What has handles and flies?
A witch in a dustbin.

😊

Which monster is green and stroppy?
The Incredible Sulk.

😊

What is Count Dracula's favourite fruit?
The necktarine.

😊

Did you hear about the lazy skeleton?
He was bone idle.

Who cleans a haunted school?
A scaretaker.

What do you get when a dinosaur sneezes?
Out of the way!

What do you call a chicken that goes
bump in the night?
A poultrygeist.

Why do dragons sleep during the day?
So they can fight knights.

Who won the monsters' beauty contest?
No one.

What do you call a dinosaur that
never gives up?
Try-try-try-ceratops.

What do you call a nervous witch?
A twitch.

Why couldn't the ghost order a vodka
at the bar?
They didn't serve spirits.

Where do you find a cemetery?
In the dead centre of town.

How does a monster count to 17?
On his fingers!

Where do ghouls go swimming?
Lake Eerie.

What do you call a haunted policeman?
Inspectre.

How do ghosts send letters overseas?
By scaremail.

How do ghosts begin business letters?
"Tomb it may concern..."

What goes "WOO-HA-HA" THUMP?
A monster laughing his head off.

☺

What type of coffee does a vampire drink?
De-coffin-ated.

☺

What do cannibals eat on toast?
Baked beings.

☺

What do you do with a green monster?
Wait until it's ripe.

☺

What do you feed an invisible cat?
Evaporated milk.

☺

Why didn't the witch wear a flat cap?
There was no point.

What is the Abominable Snowman's
favourite meal?
Spag-yeti.

Where do stinky witches get washed?
In a hubble bubble bath.

How can you tell when there's a
giant monster under your bed?
When your nose touches the ceiling.

Did you hear about the incredibly
clever monster?
He was called Frank Einstein.

How do you describe a smelly witch with heaps
of gold stashed away in her cauldron?
Stinking witch.

What do you call a skeleton who can't
be bothered to get out of bed?
Lazy bones.

Where do ghosts swim?
In the Dead Sea.

Why are ghosts dreadful liars?
You can always see through them.

What's Dracula's favourite soup?
Scream of mushroom.

What sport do vampires play?
Batminton.

What's a ghost's favourite party game?
Musical bumps in the night.

Which monster is the best dancer?
The boogieman.

Did you hear about the man that
used to be a werewolf?
He's all right now-wow-wooooooooo!

How did the boy know what the
ghost was getting for Christmas?
He felt his presents.

What did the Loch Ness Monster
say to the salmon?
"Long time, no sea."

Why couldn't the frightened archer
hit the target?
Because his arrows were all in a quiver.

Did you hear about the witch's
enormous mixing pot?
It was called Ron.

Did you hear about the witch's breakfast cereal?
It went snap, cackle and pop.

Why couldn't the skeleton go to the disco?
He had no body to dance with.

Why do demons and ghouls get on so well?
Because demons are a ghoul's best friend.

What does a wet-weather witch do?
She forecasts rainy spells.

What do you do with a blue monster?
Try to cheer it up.

I have a large, hooked nose,
three eyes and cabbages for ears.
What am I?
Really ugly.

Did you hear about the horribly hungry
monster who ate a sofa and two armchairs?
He had a three-piece-suite tooth.

Did you hear about the banshee who
wanted to be an actress?
She did a scream test.

Who lights up a haunted house?
The lights witch.